Foreword

We like the looks of playing cards so much that we decided it would be fun to devote this whole book to using them, either to make artist trading cards (ATCs), greeting cards, journals or albums in which to hold the cards. Playing cards are not just colorful and fun, they're also very accessible. Who doesn't have a pack of playing cards in the bottom of a drawer or put away with the Scrabble and Monopoly games?

And, of course, the playing cards are just the right size and weight for creating artist trading cards. which are always 2½" x 3½". Several ATCs are showcased starting on page 12.

Artist trading cards are little works of art that you can make and trade with others. The nice thing about ATCs is you don't really have to be an artist to make them. Honest.

You can look through the pages of this book to get inspiration and then just take off and create a tiny masterpiece all your own.

There are lots of sites on the internet where you can join trades (see page 3). People all over the world are involved. Or, you can create your own group and trade with each other. However you decide to trade, you'll find that this is a fun and addictive hobby.

This book provides basic information about making the artist trading cards, greeting cards, boxes, journals and albums. A variety of playing cards, game cards and sometimes an original playing card was used. Each project has an instruction and in many cases, the source of the supplies used. Special techniques are explained starting on page 48.

Several images from our collection of ephemera can be found on pages 53 to 61. Use these images and your imagination to make your own unique cards.

Practice the techniques, relax, and enjoy the creative process. Then let your own personality shine on your cards. Remember, anyone can be an artist.

Table of Contents

About Trading Cards

What are trading cards?

Sports trading cards were first produced in the 1880s by tobacco and chewing gum manufacturers. Trading these cards became a favorite hobby of millions of Americans.

"Trade" cards which were manufactured in the late 19th century were used to advertise products. They weren't meant to be traded, but were collected and most typically pasted in scrapbooks.

So how did artist trading cards come about? The original concept was developed in Switzerland by M. Vanci Stirnemann. In 1996 he produced 1200 handmade cards to document his activities with other artists. At an exhibition of these cards visitors to the gallery were encouraged to create their own cards to trade with Vanci and others at the close of the exhibit. Since then trading sessions have taken place there every month. ATCs have since been made and traded around the world.

There are several internet sites devoted to making and trading ATCs such as:

artchixstudio.com (click on "Swaps")
papercraftsmag.com (click on "Swaps")
artisttradingcards.meetup.com
artist-trading-cards.ch
art-e-zine.co.uk/atcwings.html

On the following pages are ideas for albums and boxes that can be used to store your cards. These projects would also make ideal gifts for friends or family members.

Card Swaps

Card swaps are a fun way to share your artwork with others and enjoy theirs in return. It's easy to set up a trading club. Get some friends together who you think will enjoy making cards. Maybe you have a friend who's a scrapbooker, a rubber stamper, or one who paints or draws. Actually, anyone can be a trading card artist.

You'll need work surfaces for everyone and group members should bring along their supplies. You might want to provide some refreshments, play inspiring music and provide good lighting. Then it's time to create.

After the cards are made, it's trading time. This can be done in several ways. You could number the cards and put numbers in a hat for each person to draw. Or each person makes cards to equal the number of people in the group. Everyone gets an equal amount of cards.

Another way is for the members of the group to make their cards at home and bring them to the meeting for trading. You can use the meetings to share new techniques, tools and supplies.

Your group might decide they want to trade with another group in another state or a foreign country. Check the internet for other groups or individuals who would be interested. There are card traders all over the world.

Diamonds Forever

Cover a journal with gold embossed calligraphy paper (K and Company). Glue a burgundy and gold diamond print ribbon over the spine. Using gold ink, stamp a diamond image (#3218F Rubber Stampede) on black paper cut in a diamond shape. Edge the black diamond with a gold leafing pen (Krylon). Stamp the same image around the edge of the Queen card in gold ink. Paint the Queen card with red Twinkling H2Os as pictured. Layer the card over the diamond and glue to the journal. Attach pewter brads (#23720 Making Memories) to the diamond paper. Stamp "JOURNAL" to the burgundy paper using alphabet stamps (LL#406 Hero Arts) in black ink. Glue this over a slightly larger black cardstock. Apply this to the journal along with gold photo corners.

Flights of Fancy

Cover the left edge of the journal with calligraphy paper. Cover the spine with black/white check ribbon. Glue the ribbon also to the center, front of the journal. Antique four playing cards using a beige ink stamp pad. Glue the cards to the journal as pictured. Cut the photo (page 57) in an oval shape and dot around it using gold puff paint (Tulip). Cut an image of butterfly wings in half and glue to each side of the photo. Glue the gold charm to the lower section of the journal. Glue two lengths of black/white check ribbon to the inside front and back covers of the journal and tie to close.

Remember When

Glue corrugated paper to the spine of a composition book. Cut dot paper (#10006 Daisy D's) using pinking shears and glue to the book. Glue a torn piece of black paper to the center. Stamp "JOURNAL" (#E3-516 Stampers Anonymous) using brown ink stamp pad on beige paper. Tear around it and glue to the black paper. Glue Queen images to photo mounts and glue to the journal as pictured. Glue the "remember when" ribbon (7 Gypsies) to the journal along with buttons to each photo mount.

Travel Memories

Glue a copy of a map on the cover of a journal. Stamp the woman image (Inkadinkado) on ecru tissue paper. Tear around the image. Brush decoupage medium (Mod Podge) on the tissue paper and apply to map. Decoupage another sheet of tissue paper on the cover. Photocopy and reduce images of playing cards and travel stickers. Decoupage card copies to journal as pictured. Cut out wording for travel destinations (from computer type or magazines) and tear around the edges. Glue them randomly to the album. Decoupage another sheet of tissue paper all over the cover. Rub gold ink on the edges of the journal. Glue a length of ribbon to the cover.

My Card Album

Cover a three ring binder with purple mulberry paper. Cut a piece of lavender checked paper (#61167 Memories in the Making) in a triangle and glue to the cover as pictured. Tear lavender mulberry paper into circles. Glue to the cover. Affix round letters (#20931 Eyelet Tag Alphabet by Making Memories) in each circle of mulberry paper. Tear another piece of lavender mulberry paper a little larger than a card. Glue to cover. Glue photo corners to the paper spaced to hold your favorite trading card.

Plastic sheets made to hold sports cards are perfect for displaying and safeguarding your ATCs. They fit nicely in a 3-ring binder (see left).

Kim's Cards

Glue a strip of black fleece fabric to the spine of the black/white check album. Glue the letters (Classic Font Alphabet Charms by Making Memories) to the top of the album and the joker card to the bottom. Glue the metal photo corners (#22722 Charmed by Making Memories) to each corner of the card. Wrap silver thread around the black fleece section of the cover in a random fashion and glue on the inside of album to secure.

Baby's First Years

Prepare the doll: Make a copy of the girl (page 57). Cut the dress part to fit a domino and glue on. Cut out the face and glue to a round button. String assorted beads on thread for the legs and glue to the bottom of the domino. String beads and safety pins on thread for the arms. Glue on each side of domino using a strong glue. Set aside.

Use a sponge dauber and green ink stamp pad to color the playing card. Cut pink cardstock a bit larger than the card using decorative scissors. Cover the album with the print paper (#AG128 Anna Griffin) just on the right side leaving the binding exposed. Glue pink/white check ribbon to the edge of the paper. Wrap the ribbon around and glue to the inside of the cover. Layer the pink cardstock and card and glue to the front of the album. Glue the doll body to the card. Glue the button to the card with a spacer underneath (we used another button for a spacer).

Rub calligraphy paper and playing cards with Pearlescent Beige ink pad (Tsukineko). Use decoupage medium (Mod Podge) and sponge brush to cover the frame with torn pieces of calligraphy paper and the cards. When dry, turn over and trim edges with a craft knife. Tear strips of calligraphy paper and affix to the edges of the frame, over the cards. Cover with a final coat of decoupage medium. Glue on the corner charms using jewelry glue.

For the framed image: Enlarge a black club on copy machine. Cut out vintage family images (page 55, or use your own family photos) to fit in the circles of the club. Glue on and then glue this to a piece of calligraphy paper. Insert in frame.

Deco-Cards

Make copies of face cards placing them close together on the copier. Put the copy through a shredder. Don't worry about keeping the images in order. Leave the strips long, as you'll be trimming them later. With a sponge brush, apply a layer of decoupage medium to one part of the molding of the black frame. Glue the strips a few at a time on an angle to the frame. A tweezers comes in handy for this process. Keep adding medium to the other sections of the frame and continue adding strips until the frame is covered. When dry, turn the frame over on the table and trim the strips using a craft knife. Add another application or two of decoupage medium. Insert a photograph of your choice. Paint the wooden beads black and hot glue (or use wood glue) to the bottom edge of the frame.

Anyone for Cards

Enlarge Queen and King cards to a jumbo size. Cut the Queen and King in oval shapes and decoupage to the top and sides of a cigar box. Cut out the large suit symbols and randomly decoupage them as pictured. Brush another coat of decoupage medium over the images and the whole box. When dry, apply Diamond Glaze (JudiKins) over the King oval. Two or three applications may be needed. When dry, do the same over the Queen image. Paint four large wooden beads red. Glue round game pieces (could also be checkers) to the bottom four corners of the box and then the red beads using a strong glue.

Fit for a Queen

Brush leafing size on the wooden box. When it feels tacky, apply the variegated leaf flakes with a soft brush. Brush off excess flakes. Cut the card and suit transparencies (Design Originals). Apply the card to the center of the box using decoupage medium which dries clear. Apply the suit pieces to square pebbles (Bits and Baubles by Creative Imaginations). Apply them to each side of the card using decoupage medium.

Artist's Card Box

Cover a box with calligraphy paper. Cut black craft
foam or cardstock in triangles and glue to each corner.
Glue copies of red suit symbols on each black corner.
Make copies of favorite artists and glue their faces over
the face cards. Copy their names (from art books or
printed from the computer) and tear around the edges,
then glue to the cards. Glue other suit symbols to the
top of the box as pictured. Glue a brass button to the
front of the box.

Gallery of ATCs

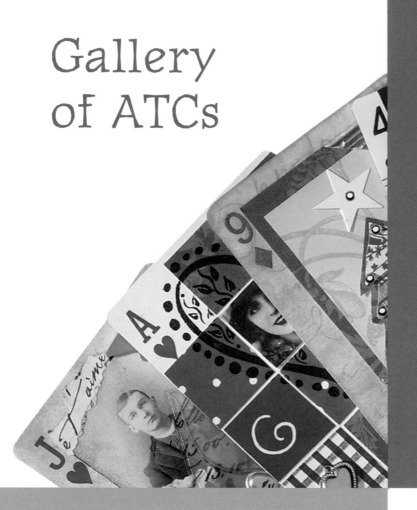

Using playing cards to make ATCs

The following are helpful tips:

Playing cards are slick and inks tend to smudge. If you're going to use rubber stamping for your design, make photocopies of the cards.

To use the real card, use Stazon ink pads. Wait 3 - 5 minutes until the ink dries. Or you can use the embossing technique (see page 48) for a permanent image. You can always use the real card if you're doing a collage design with no stamping.

If you use a photocopy of the card, back it with cardstock to make it heavy enough. If using any of the special techniques on your cards, practice them first on pieces of scrap paper.

Trio

Make two reductions of the card. Rub the different colored stamp pads over the cards with a circular motion (we used peach, lavender, green, pink and blue pigment brush pads by Color Box). Stamp all over the cards with the ornamental images (#2403R All Night Media) and purple ink. Cut blue and lavender cardstock slightly larger than the cards and round the corners. Glue the cards to the cardstock. Use spacers between the cards and glue the cards together.

Note: Use sticky notes to mask areas on the card and then rub alternately with lavender, peach, blue, and green ink stamp pads forming a grid pattern.

Royal Couple

Use sticky notes to make grids (see note at left). Stamp with decorative borders (Anna Griffin) and ornamental image (#2403R All Night Media). Cut out copies of King and Queen faces. Decorate their headgear with gold glitter glue (Sparkles). Enlarge the "club" and cut it out in a square shape. Rub the corners with the same colors used on the card. Attach it on an angle using a spacer. Add glue to the King and Queen and slip them under the square. Glue a purple jewel in the center of the "club".

Jack With a Box

Rub a Jack of diamonds with bright colored ink stamp pads. Cut a piece of white cardstock $1\frac{1}{4}$" x 5". Fold it accordion style into four pages. Cut red, blue, purple and gold cardstock $1\frac{1}{4}$" square. Glue these to the white cardstock on the other panel, front and back. Cut a $\frac{3}{4}$" square in the first panel, $\frac{1}{2}$" diamond in the second panel and $\frac{3}{8}$" square in the third panel and a $\frac{1}{4}$" diamond in the fourth panel. Fold this up and glue the back of the last panel to the middle of Jack.

13

Here's an example of a series of ATCs. We loved this photograph of the two guys in their odd uniforms. The photograph was actually a postcard with a funny inscription: "Hello Mother. Here is Walter and his partner as they pack lime. Don't you think it good?". It was so much fun to create these six different cards using the same photograph. You might want to try creating your own series. Select this photograph (page 57) or another from our ephemera pages and then find words or letters in magazines that fit the photograph. See what you can come up with.

Two Tone

Trace a card shape on the stripe paper (#AG036 Anna Griffin) and cut out. Glue to a card or cardstock. Cut out the photo and glue to the card. Stamp "2" in two corners. Make copies of spades and glue next to the "2s". Cut out desired wording from a magazine and glue over the photo.

Never Stop Glowing

Trace a card shape on the blue and gold dot paper (Shizen). Cut out and glue to a card or cardstock. Cut out the photo and glue to the card. Glue desired words to the top of the card. Glue the five silver stars around the top of the photo as pictured.

Road Warriors

Trace a card shape on the dot paper (#10006 Daisy D's) and cut out. Glue to a card or cardstock. Cut out pictures of desired motorcycles or cars and glue to the card. Cut out the photos of men and glue them by the vehicles. Cut out desired wording and glue to the top of the card.

Beauty and Brains

Trace the card shape on the lavender paper (#AG031 Anna Griffin) and cut out. Glue to the card or cardstock. Cut out the copy of the photo using deckle edge scissors. Apply photo corners to the photo and glue to the center of the card. Cut wording of your choice from a magazine (or print from computer) and glue across the photo. Glue the cherub under the wording. Stamp "2" in black ink on two corners.

Prada - Armani

Trace the card shape on the houndstooth paper (#61022 Memories in the Making). Glue it to a card or cardstock. Cut around the photo. Stamp the heart in red ink randomly to the card. Copy the "2" and hearts from a playing card and cut out. Glue to the card as pictured. Glue desired words from a magazine to top of card as pictured.

Send in the Clowns

Trace the card shape on the bubble paper (#61076 Memories in the Making) and cut out. Glue to a card or cardstock. Use a brass alphabet stencil to add the "2s" in each corner as pictured (or use a rubber stamp). Make copies of spades and glue next to the 2s. Cut the desired wording using deckle edge scissors and glue to the card.

15

Imagine

Trace the card on the gold handmade paper and cut out. Cut one corner of the paper using decorative scissors to expose the number on the card. Glue paper to the card. Glue the black/white check ribbon over the paper and the strip of torn calligraphy across the bottom. Paint the button by drizzling Pinata Inks (Sangria, then Calabaza Orange) to give a tortoise effect. Allow to dry. Cut the photo (page 55) in a circle a bit smaller than the button. Glue it to the center of the button. Glue the button to the card over the ribbon.

Queen of the Nile

Edge the Queen playing card with the gold leafing pen (Krylon). Rub the edge with gold glitter glue (Sparkles). Cut a piece of laminate sheet (JudiKins) to fit the center of the card. Place variegated leaf flakes in a paper plate and press the adhesive side of the laminate sheet into the flakes. Brush off the excess flakes until the sheet is covered. Glue the sheet to the card. Glue a copy of an Egyptian Queen (page 59) to a small piece of craft foam. Cut out around the Queen and glue to the center of the card.

From the Window

Antique a Queen of Clubs card with beige ink stamp pad. Cut a piece of cardstock to fit the middle of the card. Paint it with gold Paper Paint (Delta). Paint over this with Crackle Medium (Delta). When dry, but still slightly tacky, paint over it with rust paint. The paint will crack. Glue to card. Glue photo (ArtChix) to a piece of black craft foam. Edge with gold leafing pen (Krylon). Cut the two shutters also from black craft foam. Outline and add lines with a gold leafing pen. Glue them to the sides of the window.

La Dama

Stamp the Frida image (#1996 A Stamp in the Hand) on a piece of silver foil using pigment ink. Emboss with gold powder and heat gun. Cut around the foil using scallop edge scissors. Cut gold corrugated paper (Shizen) 2½" x 3". Fold each edge in about 1" to form the doors. Glue to the center of the card. Glue the embossed foil to the center of the corrugated. Cut a small triangle of the gold corrugated and glue to the top as pictured. Dot around the edge of the card with pink glitter glue (Sparkles) and a purple dot at the top.

Charmed, I'm Sure

Tear strips of gold and blue marbled wrapping paper. Glue one strip across the card on an angle and the other strips to the top and bottom. Edge the sides of the card with turquoise ink. Heat a strip of black craft foam with a heat gun and press a decorative stamp into the design to emboss it. With a cotton swab, rub lavender Pearl Ex powder on the design. Outline the spades with gold puff paint (Tulip), then dot the embossed design with the gold. Glue the photo of lady (page 59) to a piece of cardstock and cut in an oval. Outline the oval with gold glitter glue (Sparkles). Glue a small heart charm to the photo and then glue the oval over the embossed foam.

Queen of Klundberg Clothing

Cut out the photo (page 55). Cut blue paper to fit the center section of the card. Glue it to the card. Stamp all over with a decorative image (#TC51 Foliate Quad Cube by Stampendous) and lavender ink stamp pad. Stamp "Q's" (alphabet by Susan Branch for All Night Media) on lavender cardstock. Cut into small strips and glue to the card covering the "Q's" on the card. Glue the cut out photo to the card. Glue jewels to the right edge of card.

Promises

Stamp a Queen card with Ornate Archway (ST5-103-E Postmodern Design) and burgundy ink. Cut out the image (ArtChix) using decorative scissors and glue to card at a slight angle. Glue the gold stars across the photo and the charm (Creative Beginnings) to the upper right corner. Glue "promises" calligraphy to brass plaque (#66515 Memories in the Making) and sew onto the card using gold thread (Kreinik).

We Are Five

Antique the card by brushing on tea dye ink (Paper Plus by Delta). Stamp the card with a "5" stamp and pigment ink. Emboss with gold powder and heat gun. Sew the "5" charm to the center of the card. Make a copy of the photo (page 59) and cut around it. Glue to the bottom of the card and trim to fit.

Pulling it Together

Trace the card shape on the calligraphy paper (#61225 Memories in the Making) and cut out. Glue to a card or cardstock. Make a copy of the photo (page 55) and put it through a shredder. Line up the strips and using a tweezer, glue each strip on the card. Press the "Q" stickers (#64050 Memories in the Making) to each corner.

Be-Ribboned

Stamp calligraphy (#25971 JudiKins) in black ink on the 2" wide green ribbon. Glue a small photo (ArtChix) to cardstock and cut in a circle (smaller than the button). Glue to the center of the button. Drizzle Diamond Glaze (JudiKins) over the top of the photo. Apply 2 or 3 more times, allowing to dry between applications. Trace a card shape on the floral paper (#AG112 Anna Griffin) and cut out. Glue it to the bottom part of the card. Place the ribbon over the top and fold around to the back, gluing to secure. Glue the button to the center of the ribbon. Cut out a part of the flower from the same paper and glue over the top of the ribbon.

I Love Presents

Stamp woman image (#BLI-105-C Postmodern Design) on pink paper. Cut in an oval and glue to the card. Stamp "u" beside the "4" on the card. Stamp "I love Presents" (#66620 Thinkable Inkables by Memories in the Making) on the top of card. Make a small bow of black ribbon and glue to the hat. Glue three small pearls on the woman's ear. Lightly rub a pink stamp pad around the edge of the card.

Tip

Incorporate the numbers and letters on the cards in your designing as we did here. Other examples can be found on pages 31, 33 and 40.

Patchwork Greeting

Age a card by rubbing it with a pink stamp pad. Cut a 2" square of pink cardstock and glue to the center of the card. Cut 12 - ½" squares of various coordinating papers (Memories in the Making and Anna Griffin) and glue nine to the pink cardstock as pictured. Cut the other three in half diagonally and glue these triangles to the top and bottom of the quilt. "Sew" white embroidery floss ties to the center of the quilt. Glue the scissors charm and the spools to the card as pictured.

Artful

Stamp the card with background image (#2231 Hampton Art Stamp) on an angle using red ink stamp pad. Cut red floral paper (#AG050 Anna Griffin) using decorative scissors and glue to two corners. Cut a strip of calligraphy paper using decorative scissors and glue to the middle of the card on an angle.

The Secret Victoria

Cut out a fashion illustration (of choice) and glue to the middle section of the card with the Queen's head exposed. Stamp around the edge of the card with a decorative leaf image (#TC51 Foliate Quad Cube by Stampendous) and pink ink stamp pad. Cut out a hat and glue to the Queen's head. Add a jewel and feather to the hat. Add jewels to the Queen's straps.

Moon Glow

Glue calligraphy paper (#AG040 Anna Griffin) to the center part of the card. Use a sponge dauber and Distress Ink (Ranger) to antique the card. Edge the card with a gold leafing pen (Krylon). Cut copy of the photo (page 59) with deckle edge scissors. Glue to the center of the card. Glue the ribbon to the top left of card. Punch a hole in the left side and thread gold ribbon through the moon charm then through the hole in the card. Glue or tape on the back to secure. Glue the gold and black beads randomly to the right side of the card.

Blue Moon

Trace a card shape on the black paper and cut out. Cut across the top left edge using decorative scissors to expose the number on the card. Glue to card. Use a sponge dauber and pink ink to add color to the card. Glue photo (ArtChix) to back of photo mount (Design Originals). Drizzle Diamond Glaze over the photo in two or three applications, allowing to dry between each application. When still wet, shake on a small amount of silver glitter. When dry, glue the mount to the card. Cut out magazine letters to spell "Blue Moon" and glue to the top of the card. Glue the stars randomly to card.

23

Two's Company

Trace card shape on the gold paper (K and Company) and cut out. Glue the paper to the card. Cut out around the photo (page 55) and glue to the card. Glue a piece of calligraphy paper to the lower left. Stamp a "2" to dot paper (#10006 Daisy D's). Tear and glue to the lower right. Glue the "2" from number paper (#1939 by 7 Gypsies) to upper left. Make copies of spades (large and small) and rub with brown ink stamp pad and glue to the card as pictured. Wrap gold thread (Kreinik) around the center of the card and tape or glue on the back to secure.

Friend

Tear a piece from a page of an old book and glue to the card exposing the "2's." Glue the black/white check ribbon down the center. Trim end of ribbon as pictured. Place the square pebble (Creative Imaginations) on cardstock and trace around it. Cut out the square. Adhere bits of decorative paper, the vintage photo (page 59) and a scrap of calligraphy to the adhesive back of the pebble. Glue the pebble to the decorated cardstock in the center of the ribbon. Glue on a teapot charm (#66554 Memories in the Making).

Love Letters

Antique the card using Walnut Ink (Paper & Ink Arts). Trace the card shape on the back of the gold print paper (Shizen). Tear one edge of the paper and age it by painting Walnut Ink along the torn edge. Glue this piece to the card leaving the top edge open. Cut a piece of calligraphy paper and glue it to a piece of cardstock. Press a postage stamp sticker (#64188 Memories in the Making) to the top. Glue the photo (page 59) to the bottom area. Tie this with gold thread (Kreinik). Place in the pocket along with a small feather. Glue the key and lock charms (Memories in the Making) to the lower right.

I Am Queen

Prepare a microscope slide: Stamp the face image (Magenta #170716) on the slide using pigment ink. Emboss with purple powder and heat gun. Edge the glass using copper foil.

For the card: Brush the card with tea dye ink (Paper Plus by Delta). When dry, edge with a bronze leafing pen (Krylon). Glue photo (page 57) to left side of card. Glue a small piece of calligraphy to bottom right side of card. Glue the slide over the card so that the calligraphy shows through.

Lucky Seven

Glue a strip of green print vellum (#61l63 Memories in the Making) down the center of the card and a torn strip of green mulberry paper across the vellum. Glue a square of black cardstock to the center. Stamp vine heart (#C3609 Santa Rosa) on a piece of 36 gauge silver foil (American Art Clay) using black ink stamp pad. Fill in the design with green paint. Cut out around the design and glue to the black square. Cut two triangles of tin using decorative scissors and glue to the top and bottom of the black square. Glue on two small green beads.

Autumn Haze

Rub the card with green ink stamp pad. Stamp leaves to edges of card using olive green ink. Glue on a natural dried fern. Stamp the tree (Nature's Silhouettes by Hero Arts) on beige paper with blue ink stamp pad. Cut out and glue to a larger piece of black cardstock and a torn square of green mulberry paper. Glue to the center of the card with a spacer in between.

Knighted

Make a copy of the Jack of spades card. Paint various parts of Jack using assorted colors of Twinkling H2Os. Color in the spade using purple glitter glue (Sparkles). Edge the card with a silver ink stamp pad. Cut out a horizontal section in the center of the card and glue a piece of metal mesh (American Art Clay) to the back of the card. Outline the opening with gold glitter glue. Glue blue paper on the back of the mesh. Glue crown (page 59) to Jack's head. Fill in parts of the design with glitter glue (Sparkles).

Five of Diamonds

Stamp diamond pattern (#3218F Rubber Stampede) with purple ink on the card. Rip red/white gingham paper napkin and place in two corners. Glue on two corners of red spiral paper (#61154 Memories in the Making) over the gingham. Reduce the 5 of diamonds card. Glue it to a background of red spiral paper cut slightly larger with the corners rounded. Glue a spacer to the large card and glue the small card to this. Add a purple jewel to the center.

Soulmates

Make copies of the photo and illustration (page 55). Cut around both using deckle edge scissors and glue to the card as pictured. Glue a list of names to a small piece of craft foam and cut into a small square. Glue to the card. Add the colored brads (#22395 Making Memories) to the photo. Stamp "Soulmates" (Thinkable Inkables by Memories in the Making) using pigment ink. Emboss with purple embossing powder and heat gun. Stamp "Girl's Rule" (Memories in the Making) and emboss with turquoise embossing powder and heat gun. Glue the charms (#66550 Memories in the Making) to the bottom part of the card.

Groovy Gals

Paint the card using green Twinkling H2Os. Stamp the edge of the card with the leaves (#TC51 Foliate Cube from Stampendous) and green ink. Make a copy of the ladies (page 59) and cut around with a decorative edge scissors. Glue to the center of the card. Paint the "Great Outdoors" ribbon (7 Gypsies) with the same green paint and glue to the bottom edge of the card. Glue the charm (#66561 Memories in the Making) to the top of the photo. Stamp "Groovy Gals" (Thinkable Inkables by Memories in the Making) to top of the card.

Drama Queen

Stamp a piece of white paper with heart background stamp (#S-1584 Hero Arts) and red ink. Cut it to fit the center of the Queen of Hearts card and glue in place. Stamp the child image (Artchix) on paper and cut out using deckle edge scissors. Glue on the heart paper. Cut out an image of a crown (page 59). Glue to child's head and color in with gold glitter glue (Sparkles). Glue small jewels to crown. Punch two small holes in the bottom part of card and thread jump rings through. Attach gold stars through the jump rings. Outline the card with gold leafing pen (Krylon). Stamp "Drama Queen" (Thinkable Inkables by Memories in the Making) on each edge of the card in black ink.

Doggone Cute

Use the copy of the game card (page 59). Glue to a piece of cardstock. Edge the cardstock with a gold leafing pen (Krylon). Stamp the "swirl" image in black ink around the edge of the card. Add the "d" (#21158 ColorBok) and "g" (#21826 Scrap Essentials) brads to the card on each side of the "O". Punch a hole in the center, bottom of the card. Thread a jump ring through and add a dog charm.

Far East

Rub a gold ink stamp pad over the card. Stamp Chinese characters (Hero Arts # C1767) around the edge of the card and on a red strip of paper. Glue the strip to the center of the card. Fold a piece of printed Japanese paper into a fan and glue onto the card. Glue a charm in the upper right corner.

Note

Always remember to sign and date your cards and if you'd like, add your address, phone number, email address or website to the back of each card that you trade.

Composer Medley

Trace a playing card on the back of a copy of sheet music and cut out. Glue on the card, exposing the numbers. Cut strips of red and black cardstock and red print paper (#AG095 Anna Griffin). Layer and glue to the card as pictured. Stamp the composers (Composer Cube #MS2-101-G Postmodern Design) on a sheet of white paper with black ink. Reduce the images and cut out. Glue to a black strip and cover each one with a square pebble (Creative Imaginations).

ATC Greeting Cards

Get Well Card

Ailing?

Cut out the illustrations (page 61) in squares. Glue a torn piece of black cardstock to the center top of the card and the illustrations as pictured. Glue two torn pieces of houndstooth paper (#61021 Memories in the Making) to the upper right and lower left. Stamp "iling" after the "A" of the card using alphabet stamps and black ink. Stamp "feel better" on torn paper at the bottom of the card. Punch small holes around the edge of card. Use a needle and black thread to sew around the card. Knot thread on the back and glue or tape to secure.

Bouquet

Trace a card shape on lavender paper (AG031 Anna Griffin) and cut out. Glue to a card or cardstock. Stamp "Q" (Vintage Alphabet, Hero Arts) in blue ink to top left corner. Rub gold ink around the edge of the card. Cut out a woman image of your choice and glue to upper right corner of card. Glue a torn piece of lavender mulberry paper below woman. Cut a small piece from a paper doily and wrap into a cone. Glue along the edge to secure. Wrap a length of lavender ribbon around the cone and tie in a bow. Glue the cone to the card. Glue tiny pearls as a necklace. Place tiny straw flowers in the cone and glue in place.

Mother's Day or
Birthday Card

Valentine ATC Cards

Hearts Aplenty

Cut four different red patterned papers (Memories in the Making and Anna Griffin) into nine - $3/4$" squares. Cut a vintage face image (ArtChix) into $3/4$" squares. Glue all the squares to the cards as pictured (except the face). Stamp with the heart image (#G-2541 Santa Rosa) and black ink. Glue on the face. Add a heart charm in the lower left square.

Valentine Jack

Paint the card with Walnut Ink. Cut a face from a vintage photo (page 55) and glue over Jack's face. Cut a piece of red gingham paper-backed fabric and glue bottom and sides to bottom of card leaving the top open to form a pocket. Paint red rickrack with Walnut Ink to age. Glue to top of pocket. Tear a strip of calligraphy and glue over the red gingham. Cut out a heart from a sheet of calligraphy, edge with a gold leafing pen (Krylon). Glue on a small flower. Tuck the heart into the pocket. Glue on a heart charm.

Out on a Limb

Cut the photo (page 55) and the red floral paper (AG050 Anna Griffin) a bit larger using deckle edge scissors. Layer and glue to the card. Use a sponge dauber and pink ink to add color to the edges of the card. Use lettering from a postcard or magazine "My Valentine" to glue after the "4" on the card. Type lettering "I'd go out on a limb for you" on computer. Cut out using deckle edge scissors and glue over photo. Glue cherub sticker to upper right.

Je T'aime

Antique the card using a sponge dauber and Distress Ink (Ranger). Glue the photo (page 59) to the center of the card along with the gold photo corner (#SPJD #003 Jolee's Boutique) on the upper right edge. Cut words from magazine or print from computer "Je T'aime" and "Love". Glue a strip of gold tissue to the bottom part of the card. Glue the words as pictured and a picture of the Eiffel Tower. Place three heart charms in the vinyl pocket (#BSN A039 EK Success) and attach to the card.

Happy Dad's Day

Glue sheet music cover (page 61) to card on an angle. Cut several hearts from red/white dot paper (#61014 Memories in the Making) and glue to the card. Stamp hearts to edge of card using red ink. Stamp "happy dad's day" using alphabet stamps and black ink on white paper. Tear into a strip and glue it across the card. Rub the edge of the card with red ink stamp pad.

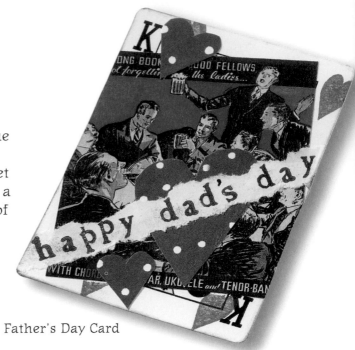

Father's Day Card

Mother's Day or Birthday Card

Mommy and Me

Cut a piece of red/white dot paper (#61014 Memories in the Making) to fit center section of card. Glue it on. Stamp the mother and daughter image (Artchix) in black ink on white paper. Cut around the image and glue to card. Stamp the vine heart (#C3609 Santa Rosa) around the edge of the card with red ink. Cut a flower from decorative paper (Anna Griffin) and glue to lower left of card. Rub the red ink stamp pad around the edge of the card.

Maestro

Trace the card shape on gold handmade paper and cut out. Tear the upper left corner to expose the "K" on the card. Glue the paper to the card. Tear a piece of the stripe paper and glue to the center of the card and a bit of calligraphy to the bottom.

Prepare the microscope slide: Cut a piece of cardstock the size of the slide. Stamp the man image (#1995-J River City Rubber Works) on a piece of brown paper. Glue this along with various papers and calligraphy and a piece of a cigar label. Press the clock sticker (#64430 Memories in the Making) to upper right. Glue this lightly to the slide. Edge the slide with copper foil. Glue the slide to the center of the card. Stamp random squares (#LL803 Hero Arts) in black ink around the card.

Father's Day or Birthday Card

34

Halloween Poetry

Brush a coat of Walnut Ink (Paper Ink) on card. Tear a piece of black mulberry paper and glue on an angle to card. Glue the postcard copy (page 61) over the black paper. Glue the poem from the postcard to gold paper and cut out using decorative scissors. Glue over the postcard and dot around with gold glitter glue (Sparkles). Fill in the "club" with gold glitter glue.

You're Invited

Glue the autumn print paper (Anna Griffin) to the card with the copy of the turkey postcard (page 61) over the top. Cut the invitation (page 61) with decorative scissors and edge with the gold leafing pen (Krylon). Glue to the center of the card. Glue a bit of torn print paper to the bottom and "Thanksgiving Day" copy over this. Glue a small feather to the bottom right of the card.

Thanksgiving Feast

Use orange and terra-cotta ink stamp pads to color the card. Stamp fruit type images using dark green ink to the top of the card. Stamp a leaf image over the top of the others using gold ink. Stamp "feast" using alphabet stamps and black ink. Apply copper foil strips in a basketweave design to bottom part of the card. Stamp a leaf image over the top in black ink. Glue two small feathers to the card.

Christmas ATC Cards

Glittering Christmas

Apply gold glitter glue (Sparkles) to the edges of the card. Glue layers of torn gold tissue and white/gold paper to the center of the card. Apply the photos (Lil Christmas photos by Artchix) to the backs of the square pebbles (Creative Imagination). Glue the pebbles to the card as pictured. Drip gold sealing wax to upper right corner and stamp with a "Merry Christmas" seal.

One French Hen

Edge a 3 of Hearts card with gold leafing pen (Krylon), then rub the edges with a lavender ink stamp pad. Cut out an image of a hen (page 61) and glue to the lower right of card. Cut out images of poinsettias (page 61) and glue to upper right and left edge as pictured. Stamp letters to spell "Noel" (Anna Griffin Alphabets) in gold ink. Glue a purple jewel to top, center of card.

Christmas Collage

Rub the playing card with a green ink pad. Cut two pieces of calligraphy paper and glue to the playing card (a triangle to upper right and a square piece to lower right). Stamp scroll image (#2403R Rubber Stampede) in red ink on white paper and rub the paper with the red ink pad. Cut to fit bottom left of card and glue on. Cut a small strip of gold calligraphy paper (K and Company) and glue over stamped piece. Cut out the poinsettia (page 61) and glue over the top of the card.

King of the Road

Stamp snowflakes randomly to the edge of the card using pigment ink stamp pad. Emboss with gold embossing powder and heat gun. Cut the Santa post card (page 61) using scallop edge scissors. Glue to a red gift tag and glue the tag to the center of the card. Punch a hole in the upper left and thread a gold thread through if using as a gift tag.

Greeting Cards

Never Show Your Cards

Fold kraft cardstock in half to form a card. Make photocopies of fanned cards. Set aside. Cut out and glue the lady (page 57) and copy which says "Never show your cards" (from computer type) to stripe paper (#61028 Memories in the Making). Cut this in a circle the same size as the optometrist lens. Carefully glue to the back of the glass. Set aside. Stamp card with the stripe image (#H2870 Hero Arts) and black ink. Outline some of the stripes with a silver leafing pen (Krylon). Glue the silver stars to one of the stripes. Age the card copies with bronze ink pad and glue to the lower right corner of the card. Trim the edges. Thread silver thread through the hole in the glass. Punch a hole in the top of the card and thread the silver thread through it and tape on the back to secure

Reflections

For microscope slide: Cut the photo of lady (page 59) using scallop edge scissors. Glue to a piece of ivory cardstock. Apply gold and pink glitter glue (Sparkles) to the photo. Glue bits of calligraphy and rosebud paper above the photo and a burgundy ribbon underneath. Lightly glue to the slide. Edge the slide with copper foil. Set aside.

Separate a toile design paper napkin until you have one thin sheet. Tear around the edge making it smaller than the card. Use Mod Podge and a sponge brush to apply to card. Edge the playing card with Distress Ink (Ranger) and glue over the top of the print napkin. Tear a piece of burgundy mulberry paper smaller than the playing card and glue over the card. Glue the slide over the mulberry paper. Tear and glue the calligraphy to corners of the card. Glue the charms (hand charm #66507 by Memories in the Making) and add postage stamp stickers as pictured. Edge the completed card with red ink.

Affectionately

Fold burgundy cardstock in half to form the greeting card. Stamp the front of the card with a large decorative stamp (#580KO2 Anna Griffin) and dark burgundy ink. Layer the card with green paper, then coral marbleized paper. Glue the playing card to this. Cut a print of a flower to fit the middle of the playing card and glue on. Tear a strip of calligraphy paper (page 57) and glue across the flower.

Butterfly Greeting

Fold burgundy cardstock in half to form the card. Stamp a large decorative stamp (#580KO2 Anna Griffin) on white cardstock with burgundy ink. Cut this to fit the front of the card and glue on. Add stickers (#64131 Memories in the Making) to the top and bottom of the card. Rub a gold leafing pen around the edge of the playing card and then glue to the stamped cardstock. Cut a butterfly sticker (#66059 Memories in the Making) to fit the middle of the playing card and glue on.

Pinwheel Birthday

Use the playing card that displays the child's age (in this case, the 5). Fold yellow cardstock in half to form the card. Layer the different colors of foil paper and glue to the card as pictured. Stamp playing card with "Happy Birthday" (Thinkable Inkables by Memories in the Making). Add dots using gold glitter glue (Sparkles). Glue on the Happy Birthday playing card. To make the pinwheels: Cut the paper in 1" squares. At each corner cut almost to the center. Pull every other corner into the center and glue. Glue a bead at the center point. Add to two corners of the card.

The New Bike

Fold red cardstock in half to form the card. Enlarge "Joker on a Bike" and make three copies. Layer two red print papers (#61006 and 61132 Memories in the Making) and a blue foil paper. Glue the playing card to this. Coat each of the "Jokers" with decoupage medium (Mod Podge) to stiffen them. When dry, cut them out and layer them with spacers in between and glue to the playing card. Punch small holes at the top of the card. Thread metallic thread through this and tie on a birthday candle.

40

You Go Girl

Fold lavender cardstock in half to form the card. Stamp the background image (Inkadinkado) on stripe paper (AG143 Anna Griffin) and cut 2¾" x 4¾" and glue to upper left corner of the card. Glue a piece of lavender stripe paper to the bottom of the card as pictured. Cut the woman's photo (page 57) and glue to upper right corner. Glue the playing card (From Touring Game, page 58) to the card along with cut out words "You" and "Girl" as pictured. Glue a white feather to lower part of card.

In Style

Make a photocopy of the playing card on brown paper and cut out. Fold brown cardstock in half to form the card. Cut striped paper (#AG036 Anna Griffin) and black paper and layer and glue to cardstock as pictured. Cut out the image of the man (page 55) Layer and glue the playing card and man's image on card. Tear small pieces of newsprint (#61098 Memories in the Making) and cut wording of choice out of a magazine. Position on card and glue (see photo). Glue button to upper right corner of card.

To Father

Glue calligraphy paper to the center of the playing card. Cut the head off of photocopy of man (page 59) and glue to a washer (or a button). Top with an application of Diamond Glaze. Let dry. Glue the photocopy of the man's body on the card. Edge the card with gold leafing pen (Krylon). Cut a crown of gold paper and glue to the top part of the card. Glue the washer over the body. Cut black cardstock in a strip. Cut the top edge using pinking shears and glue to the top part of the card. Glue "To Father" over the black strip.

For Mother

Fold purple cardstock in half to form a card. Stamp calligraphy image (#G1771 A Stamp in the Hand) in gold ink. Cut a piece of mulberry paper half the size of the card and tear along one long side to form a decorative edge. Stamp this strip using a scroll design (#2403R All Night Media) and gold ink. Glue this to the left edge of the card. Glue the trading card (see instructions page 31) to the card. Glue the heart charm to upper right corner.

You're An Angel

Glue the number paper (#1939 by 7 Gypsies) to the folded ivory cardstock. Place calligraphy paper in a glassine envelope. Seal with gold sealing wax and stamp with an alphabet seal. Glue the envelope on the top part of the card on an angle. Glue gold wings (#W105 Banar Designs) to the center of the card and the photo of lady (page 57) over the top. Glue a copy of a club to lower right corner.

Queen of Hearts

To make the center ornament: Make copies of an assortment of mini cards. Cut in a circle the size of a round tag. Glue in the center of a metal rim tag. Drizzle Diamond Glaze (Judikins) over the top in two or three applications. Let dry between each application and set aside. Edge a Queen of Hearts card with red ink. Glue the tag to the center of the playing card. Set aside.

To make the card: Fold a piece of red cardstock in half to form the card. Cut the red paper (#61132 Memories in the Making) the same size as the front of the card. Using a ruler and craft knife, make slits every $\frac{1}{2}$" around the card slightly wider than the size of the ribbon. Cut four lengths of ribbon and thread them to each edge of the card through the slits. Glue ribbon on the back of card to secure. Glue the red paper with the threaded ribbon to the card. Glue the Queen card to the center of the greeting card.

Merry Christmas

Glue the decorated playing card (see instructions on page 36) to a piece of gold corrugated and then to green paper. Apply the gold border stickers (#64027 Memories in the Making) around the outside edge of the folded card mitering the corners. Glue the playing card and layers to the center of the greeting card.

A Poinsettia Christmas

Fold ivory cardstock in half to form a card. Cut a piece of gold calligraphy paper (K and Company) the size of the front of the card and glue on. Cut a piece of cardstock smaller than the front of the card.

To make the red textured background: Mix Pattern Builder (Paper Plus by Delta) with red acrylic paint following manufacturer's instructions. Spread a light mixture on the cardstock. Stamp through the mixture using an ornamental stamp. Set aside to dry.

When dry, layer the red card and the poinsettia card (see instructions page 37) and glue to the gold card.

Star Bright

To make the tree-decorated playing card: Dab a green stamp pad over the playing card. Stamp the card with calligraphy image (#AQ-1771 A Stamp in the Hand) in gold ink. Cut a piece of red paper (#AG073 Anna Griffin) and a piece of green (#AG003 Anna Griffin) slightly smaller. Layer and glue onto the card. Cut out a Christmas tree (use a cookie cutter or stencil for a pattern) from red and white paper (#AG095 Anna Griffin). Cut a slightly larger tree from the red paper (#AG050 Anna Griffin). Layer and glue the trees onto the card. Glue two triangles of gold corrugated on two corners of the card. Glue the gold star and small crystals on the card.

To make the Christmas card: Fold a piece of ivory cardstock in half. Cut a piece of red paper (#AG115 Anna Griffin) and a piece of green (#AG003 Anna Griffin). Glue these along the folded edge of the card. Glue the tree card to the center of the card. Add a gold star and rhinestone.

Joyeaux Noel

Fold red cardstock in half to form the greeting card. Glue striped paper (AG053 Anna Griffin) to the card. Rub edges with gold leafing pen. Glue the decorated card (see instructions page 36) to the striped paper card. Cut out "Joyeux Noel" from a magazine or use computer type. Tear around the type and edge with Distress Ink (Ranger) and glue to card. Glue on a small heart charm as pictured and a gem at the top of the heart. Edge the card with the gold leafing pen.

Tools & Supplies

RUBBER STAMPS

Every image imaginable is available in rubber stamps. Some are mounted on wood, others are available in clear plexiglass for ease of positioning. Background stamps and alphabets are handy to have in your collection.

DYE INK PADS

These are available in pre-inked pads (the traditional stamp pads that you're probably familiar with). They come in a large variety of colors, are water-based and quick drying. These inks are used for stamping on all papers.

PIGMENT INK PADS

These also come in a wide variety of vivid colors. The ink is slow drying so these inks are typically used with embossing powders. The sponges on these pads sit above the base of the container so that they can be used to ink directly to any size stamp (rather than applying the stamp to the pad).

Pigment brush stamps (from Colorbox) are small oval stamp pads which can be used to decorate directly to the paper or directly to a stamp. They're easy to handle and are available in a variety of colors.

RE-INKERS

These are small bottles of dye or embossing inks that can be used to revitalize ink pads. They can also be used for watercoloring (just add a little water to the ink) or for painting directly on a stamp and then stamping onto paper. This gives you a loose, arty look.

METALLIC POWDERS

These come in a wonderful assortment of colors. The powders can be mixed with acrylics, watercolors, oils, adhesives, embossing powders and inks. Or the powders can be used right from the bottle for a chalk-like effect.

Rubber stamps

Pigment brush pads

Stamp pads, dye and pigment

Some of the many glazes and varnishes

Embossing powder

Twinkling H20s water-colors

Glitter glue

Metallic powders

Metallic acrylics

CUTTING TOOLS

Craft Knife: Has an angled blade on a cylindrical handle. Used for cutting details and clean lines.

Decorative Scissors: Many different designs are available from deckle edges to scalloped and pinked. Creates beautiful edges on paper.

Paper Punches: Hand held punches are available in several sizes and shapes.

GOLD LEAFING PENS

Leafing pens come in several different metallic shades including gold, bronze and silver. They are ideal for adding metallic borders to cards and paper. They can also be used on dark colored papers.

ADHESIVES (See gluing page 49)

The various glues used in this book:
Glue stick
Craft (white) glue
Hot glue gun and glue sticks
Industrial strength (solvent) glue

ADDITIONAL SUPPLIES

Metal ruler
Scissors
Scotch tape
Tweezers
Cotton swabs
Decorative brads
Microscope slides
Optometrist lenses

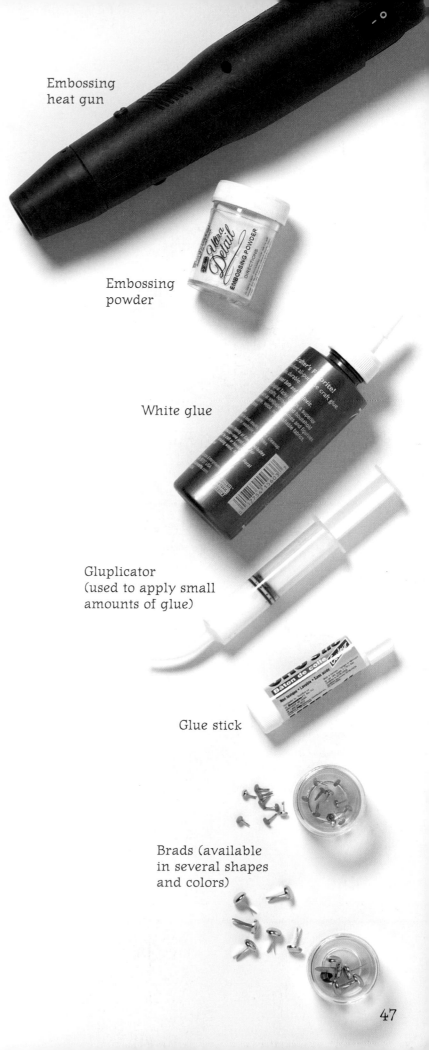

Embossing
heat gun

Embossing
powder

White glue

Gluplicator
(used to apply small
amounts of glue)

Glue stick

Brads (available
in several shapes
and colors)

Techniques

INKING A STAMP

Apply the stamp to the dye-based pad. Then stamp it on a test piece of paper. Check to make sure that it stamped completely and that you didn't get any edges from the untrimmed part of the stamp. Keep trying until you get a nice clean image. Re-ink your stamp again and stamp on your project.

Another way to ink your stamp is with a colored marker. Color the complete image area or only part of the image. Or use different color markers on the stamp for a multi-colored look.

When using extra large stamps (such as background stamps) on a small project, you can ink your stamp and place your project directly onto the stamp to ink it.

DIRECT TO PAPER INKING TECHNIQUE

Use a stamp pad with a raised pad (sometimes called "Cat's Eyes" by Color Box) to decorate the paper. Gently rub the pad onto the paper or use a sponge. You can use more than one color to create different looks.

EMBOSSING

To achieve a dimensional look to your project, stamp your design using a pigment ink stamp pad. Then impress the image onto the surface.

Pour or shake embossing powder over the wet ink. Shake off the excess.

Heat the surface using a heat gun until the powder melts and becomes raised.

You can also use a dye ink stamp pad for embossing, but this ink dries a lot faster, so you have to work much more quickly.

Try experimenting with embossing. You can use different colors of powders and metallics. You can mix colors of powders together for different effects. Embossing powders are available in different grades from detail, fine to double thick.

Embossed with gold embossing powder

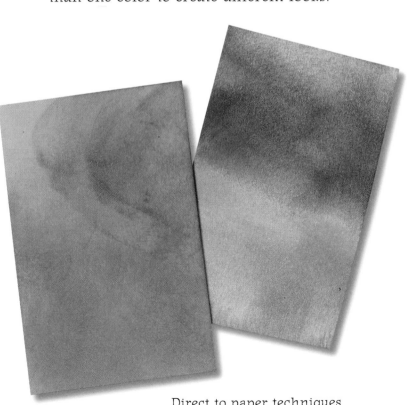

Direct to paper techniques

48

GLUING

Glue stick: UHU glue sticks work well for gluing paper to paper. The glue is rubbed to the surface of the paper. Provides a smooth, permanent bond and is acid-free.

Craft Glue: Tacky or other white glues are ideal for applying small, lightweight embellishments. They dry clear and are easy to clean up.

Hot glue gun with glue sticks: Use for applying larger items such as bows, buttons, coins and other embellishments. Not recommended for applying paper to paper because it tends to be lumpy and uneven. When using a glue gun with paper projects, a low melt gun works best.

Solvent based adhesives: Goop and Stik N Seal (Loctite) work well for adding heavy embellishments or metal items.

Diamond Glaze: A water-based dimensional adhesive that is used directly over artwork for a raised, glass-like finish. When thinned with water it has a lacquer-like finish. Dye ink can be added to it to achieve custom colors. It's also used for gluing glitter, beads, glass, plastic and vellum to paper.

DECOUPAGE

There are several products you can use for this technique including Mod Podge by Plaid, Paper Plus Decoupage Medium by Delta or Gel Medium (Matte Acrylic). With a paintbrush or foam brush, coat the surface with the medium, then place the image into the wet medium. Brush over it with another layer of the medium. Brush from the center outward. Don't worry about wrinkling or bubbles. These will usually go away when it dries.

Using the decoupage method gives you a more permanent, glossy and finished look to your work. This works well with tissue paper, other thin papers, skeleton leaves and other delicate embellishments.

Tissue paper decoupage

Diamond Glaze
on button

PASTE PAPER OR PATTERN BUILDER

A process called Paste Paper is used to add texture and dimension to paper, but making paste paper is a complicated technique. Recently Delta has come out with a product called Pattern Builder which gives a similar effect and makes the technique easy. Pattern Builder dries clear, so add paint or finish as desired. Mix colors in equal parts, adding more medium until the desired texture is achieved. You can also add glitter to the medium to achieve a sparkly effect. Apply to your card with a palette knife or plastic spatula. Use different items to rake through the medium for different textures such as a comb, fork (see below), stamp or rubber tool used for faux finishing. A rubber stamp may be stamped into the wet Pattern Builder to achieve a 3-dimensional effect (see page 44) Let dry completely.

STAINING AND AGING

There are several ways to achieve an aged look to your paper, such as:

Direct to paper: Rub on dye ink with the ink pad or your finger (golds and browns work well).

Coffee: Brush on coffee using a paintbrush. Either brush it all over the paper or brush it in streaks. The same look can be achieved using Walnut Ink Crystals by PostModern Designs, the Distress Inks from Ranger, or Paper Plus Tea Dye Varnish from Delta.

Walnut Ink: This is available as a liquid, granulated, or in a stamp pad. To use the granules, mix them with water to achieve different strengths, or sprinkle onto a wet surface to get an aged, spotty effect.

Crumpling: Crumple up the cardstock. Rub it with Walnut Ink from an ink pad. Then open up the card and smooth it out.

Pattern Builder, textured with rubber stamp

Pattern Builder, textured by combing with a fork

Crumpled cardstock rubbed with Walnut Ink pad

CRACKLING

Delta has a crackling product designed especially for paper. It's part of their Paper Plus line. To use: Apply a heavy coat of acrylic paint to the project surface. Apply a coat of crackle medium. Dry until slightly tacky. Do not dry completely. Apply another coat of acrylic paint of a contrasting color from the first coat. Cracks will begin to appear in minutes.

In the example below, we used rust colored paint as a first coat and gold as the top coat. Experiment with different colors to achieve different looks.(See page 17 for example).

USING PINATA COLORS

These dyes can be used right from the bottle and will be very saturated and brilliant or can be thinned with water. They can be brushed on like watercolors or applied with cotton swabs or sponges for a variety of different looks. Try thinning them with water and applying with an eye dropper. The different colors will overlap and spread. Tilt your paper and let the colors run together. Spattering the colors with a stiff brush would also be an interesting technique. (Be careful where you spatter!)

Card painted with rust paint, crackle medium added, then overpainted with gold

Pinata colors applied with a cotton swab

GOLD LEAF UNDER LAMINATE SHEET

Cut a piece of the laminate sheet (Judikins). Place the gold leaf flakes (can be variegated or not) on a paper plate. Remove the backing paper from the laminate sheet to expose the adhesive, then dip it adhesive-side down into the leaf flakes. Use a soft paintbrush to brush the excess leaf off, until it is flat and the whole sheet is covered. This gold leafed sheet makes a beautiful background for stamping, collage, etc.

Variegated leaf flakes
under a laminate sheet

USING PEARL EX POWDERED PIGMENTS

We liked using these right from the bottles with a cotton swab. They look much like chalk but have a metallic appearance. Spray your finished project with fixative to keep the pigments from smearing. They can also be mixed with clear embossing powder and then used with the stamped embossing technique. This way you can get several more colors then are available in embossing powders.

USING TWINKLING H2Os

These little jars pack a terrific punch. They are actually watercolors with sparkle. Spritz them with a little water and brush them either directly to paper or right onto a rubber stamp. Let it dry, then mist the stamp with water from a fine spray spritzer, then stamp the image. You can mist the stamp and use again and again.

Or your can stamp your image in the usual way, then color in the design using a small brush and the H2Os. This looks particularly good with embossed images. Because the design is raised, it's easier to stay within the lines when painting.

Twinkling H2Os
applied with a
rubber stamp

52

Sources

RUBBER STAMPS

A Stamp in the Hand
(310) 884-9700
www.astampinthehand.com

All Night Media
Plaid Enterprises
www.plaidonline.com

Anna Griffin stamps by
All Night Media
Plaid Enterprises
www.plaidonline.com

Artchix Studio
www.artchixstudio.com

Hero Arts
(510) 652-6055
www.heroarts.com

Magenta
(405) 922-5253
www.magentarubber
stamps.com

Post Modern Designs
(405) 321-3176
postmoderndesign@aol.com

River City Rubber Works
(877) 735-2276

Rubber Stampede
(800) 423-4135
www.rubberstampede.com

Stamparosa
Stampstruck
www.stampstruck.com

Stampendous
(800) 869-0474
www.stampendous.com

STAMP PADS

Clearsnap
(360) 293-6634
(pigment brush pads by Color
Box)

Ranger Crafts
www.rangerink.com
(Distress inks)

Tsukineko
www.tsukineko.com
(Versacolor and Encore
metallic stamp pads)

PAINT AND FINISHES

Delta Technical Coatings
(800) 423-4135
www.deltacrafts.com
(Paper Plus Tea Dye Vanish,
Pattern Builder, Decoupage
Medium, Crackle Finish)

Duncan Paint Company
www.duncancrafts.com
(Tulip puff paint)

Krylon
(216) 566-2000
www.krylon.com
(gold leafing pens)

Jacquard Products
(707) 433-9577
www.jacquardproducts.com
(Lumiere paints, Pearl Ex
Powders and Pinata Colors)

LuminArte
(866) 229-1544
www.luminarteinc.com
(Twinkling H2Os)

PSX
(707) 588-8058
www.psxdesign.com
(Sparkles Glitter Glue)

Paper & Ink Arts
www.paperinkarts.com
(walnut ink)

TOOLS

Fiskars
(715) 842-2091
www.fiskars.com
(decorative edge scissors,
paper punches)

EMBELLISHMENTS

American Art Clay
www.amaco.com
(foil and mesh)

ArtBar Studio
www.theartbar.net
(microscope slides &
optometrist lenses)

Artchix Studio
www.artchixstudio.com
(ephemera)

Banar Designs
(760) 728-0344
(gold wings, gluplicator)

Biblical Impressions
(877) 587-0941
www.biblical.com
(variegated leaf)

ColorBok
(734) 426-5300
www.colorbok.com
(brads)

Design Originals
www.d-originals.com
(photo mounts
& transparencies)

Judikins
(310) 515-1115
www.judikins.com
(laminate sheets and
Diamond Glaze)

Making Memories
(801) 294-0430
www.makingmemories.com
(metal alphabets, brads &
corners)

Memories in the Making
Leisure Arts
(501) 868-8800
www.leisurearts.com
(charms)

Kreinik Mfg. Co. Inc.
(410) 281-0040
www.kreinik.com
(metallic thread)

(continued)

More Sources

EMBELLISHMENTS

Scrap Essentials
www.joann.com
(metal alphabets, brads)

7 Gypsies
www.7gypsies.com
(twill ribbon)

PAPER & STICKERS

Anna Griffin, Inc.
(404) 817-8170
www.annagriffin.com

Creative Imaginations
(714) 995-2266
www.cigift.com

Daisy D's Paper Company
www.daisydspaper.com

K and Company
(816) 389-4150
www.kandcompany.com

Frances Meyer
www.francesmeyer.com

Making Memories
(801) 294-0430
www.makingmemories.com

Memories in the Making
Leisure Arts
(501) 868-8800
www.leisurearts.com

Shizen
www.shizenpaper.com

Credits

Grateful acknowledgement is made to Kim Latham of Delta Technical Coatings for her support and cooperation.

Many thanks to Jacquard Products for their cooperation with supplies for this book.

Banar Designs Principals:
Barbara Finwall and Nancy Javier
Art Direction: Barbara Finwall
Editorial Direction: Nancy Javier

Photography: Stephen Whalen
Computer Graphic Design: Dana Alison
Project Direction: Jerilyn Clements
Designs by: Jerilyn Clements, Nancy Javier,
Barbara Finwall & Kathie Morgan

Published by

LEISURE ARTS
5701 Ranch Drive
Little Rock, AR 72223
© 2005 by Leisure Arts, Inc.

Produced by

BANAR DESIGNS
P.O. Box 483
Fallbrook, CA 92088
banar@adelphia.net